Baryshnikov
in Color

Introduction and Commentaries by
MIKHAIL BARYSHNIKOV

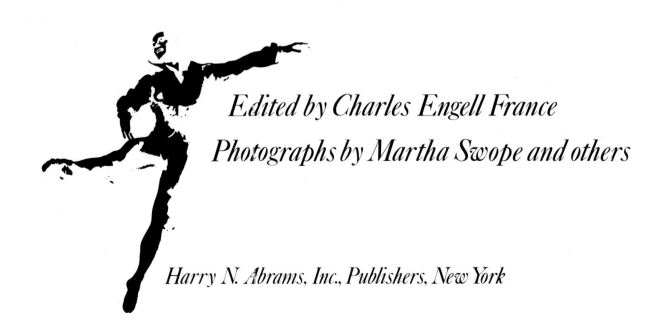

Edited by Charles Engell France
Photographs by Martha Swope and others

Harry N. Abrams, Inc., Publishers, New York

Front Cover:

Coppélia

Photograph: Steven Caras

Project Director: Darlene Geis
Designer: Gilda Kuhlman

Library of Congress Catalog Card Number: 80-66279
International Standard Book Number: 0-8109-2225-8

Text © 1980 Mikhail Baryshnikov
© 1980 Harry N. Abrams, Inc.

Printed and bound in Japan

Introduction

When I first came to America, in the summer of 1974, I knew that one of my dreams was to take advantage of the incredible variety that is a unique feature of American life. The United States has become my home and I appreciate it for all kinds of reasons, but I first came to appreciate it as a *dancer*. The memories of those early months are like the memories of childhood, when you begin to see things clearly for the first time, when you begin to grow and are aware of the growth and the pleasure it brings, of the options you will have, the sights you will see, the feelings you will feel.

I suppose that in many ways I have been the luckiest of the lucky. I landed squarely on two feet and jumped right into my dancing. There I had many, many hours of satisfying hard work with colleagues and choreographers, with designers and directors—opportunities that not many dancers are fortunate enough to have in a lifetime.

My first five years I spent happily with American Ballet Theatre (mostly) and with Britain's Royal Ballet, with occasional and very rewarding guest appearances with smaller and more experimental companies. I danced over thirty roles that were either created for me or were new versions of old classics. I then joined the New York City Ballet, where I had the extraordinary opportunity to dance many roles in the current Balanchine repertoire as well as the great works of Jerome Robbins. I also

made a Hollywood movie, *The Turning Point*, and a television special, "Baryshnikov on Broadway," in which I was able to dance an entire show made up of Broadway musical numbers.

How lucky can you get? I really have had unbelievable professional experience. I am grateful for it in a way most people cannot realize.

It began with American Ballet Theatre, a large, sprawling company with a repertoire unmatched in the world. When I arrived, the list included works by the great dramatic choreographer Antony Tudor (I later danced his *Shadowplay*), George Balanchine (I danced his *Theme and Variations*), the revolutionary Michel Fokine, who had been Diaghilev's principal choreographer (I danced his *Petrouchka* and *Le Spectre de la Rose*), and Jerome Robbins (he created *Other Dances* for me and my brilliant colleague, ballerina Natalia Makarova), as well as the time-honored classics *Giselle*, *The Sleeping Beauty*, *Coppélia*, and *La Sylphide*, among others.

But in the first three years of my stay with American Ballet Theatre, Directors Lucia Chase and Oliver Smith gave me one opportunity after another to work with new, exciting choreographers who were trying various experiments and who developed them with me. To work with a choreographer is a unique experience...a cross between the perfect vacation and being in church. Not to mention all the hard labor. I had new ballets by—among others—John Neumeier *(Hamlet Connotations)*, John Butler (*Medea*, originally created in Spoleto), and Twyla Tharp *(Push Comes to Shove)*.

What can I possibly say about my work with Twyla Tharp? That it came as a shock should come as no surprise to anyone who knows my background and who knows Twyla. Her style of movement was as foreign to me as ice to the Sahara. Brilliantly musical and brilliantly cerebral, she found a new theatrical style that evolved out of a deep understanding of classicism and its intent. But with Twyla Tharp it was changed into a new form that called for virtuosity, extremely refined musical sense, and a physicality that expressed itself in a special loose vernacular style with roots in all the theatrical dancing modes of American musicals, vaudeville, tap dancing, social dancing, and the old soft-shoe. The ballet she created for me, ballerinas Martine van Hamel and Marianna Tcherkassky, and the company was, for all of us, one of our most rewarding work experiences ever. The fact that *Push Comes to Shove* was a huge hit wasn't exactly unpleasant either.

I also created two full-length ballets for ABT in those years. Created is perhaps too strong a word. Restaged is closer to the truth. The first was *The Nutcracker*, which had beautiful scenic and costume designs by Boris Aronson and Frank Thompson. I was naturally as nervous as a cat about the whole project, and my nerves didn't get better as the premiere got closer. But the experience taught me a great deal about many aspects of living in a ballet company. As a dancer you lead—in one way or another—a very passive life. "Go here; point your foot on that count; wear this costume; time to go on stage." Your active life is the life you have as an artist, the imagination you can use, the *performance* you bring to the stage. But once you are the stager of a ballet, or the director, you have to abandon all hope of the responsibility belonging to anyone but you yourself. *You* pick the dancer, *you* pick the designer, *you* pick the form. And then the curtain goes up and the responsibility is yours, all yours.

Of course I loved doing it, too. When I came to stage my second ballet, the full-length *Don Quixote*, it was a bit easier, and I set out to have a good time. The ballet was created for Gelsey Kirkland, the most extraordinary ballerina of her generation. She brought to the leading role of Kitri her unique blend of super-refined virtuosity, lightness, bravura spirit, passion, and, perhaps most of all, her daring. I wanted this old war-horse of a ballet to be more like a lighthearted Broadway show, so I made some changes, speeded things up, and, I hope, succeeded in bringing the nineteenth century a little up to date.

During this period I also was in a Hollywood movie, *The Turning Point*. That sounds so casual, but imagine what it was like for someone used to hiding behind all the masks the theater offers a performer...all of a sudden to appear before a camera, a relentless eye from which no secrets can be concealed. *And* to speak! *And* in English! But I enjoyed the experience. I didn't become an actor, but the role was carefully tailored to my limited thespian ability and I think it came off all right. The dancing sequences were very, very beautifully photographed by Director Herbert Ross and very smoothly put together by the whole *Turning Point* team, including that extraordinary former ballerina Nora Kaye (Mrs. Herbert Ross).

My next film experience was the television special of *The Nutcracker*, performed for CBS television by Gelsey Kirkland and myself. And then a dream came true..."Baryshnikov on Broadway."

Baryshnikov on Broadway...what a thought! One of the great accomplishments of the American stage is its musicals. I have always gone to see all the musicals that open on Broadway, sitting in awe of the best Broadway dancers' talent. They have to have a kind of versatility and all-round ability that boggles the mind...they sing, they dance, they act. But how do they do it all? Well, I was offered a project by Executive Producer Herman Krawitz (who had so skillfully put together the television film of *The Nutcracker*) in which I would dance a series of Broadway numbers re-created especially for television...a salute to Broadway. Again, all the luck came my way. Choreographer Ron Field achieved wonderful evocations of many Broadway hits—and I had a fantasy fulfilled. I was a Broadway dancer. And not alone. The witty Nell Carter joined me in the show. Not to mention the cast of *A Chorus Line*. And my special guest was Liza Minnelli. Liza has heart, brains, and talent—all in great abundance and all in the right places. As Cole Porter might have said: "She's the top!" (I was a member of the chorus in the final number, Michael Bennett's original smash-hit finale from that show.)

In the period between leaving American Ballet Theatre and returning to it as the new Artistic Director in September 1980, I joined the New York City Ballet and danced more than twenty-five roles. I worked directly with George Balanchine on many roles in the unique repertoire of his masterpieces that forms the heart and soul of the New York City Ballet. I can't say enough about what it's like to work with Balanchine and to dance his ballets. It would be presumptuous in so short a space to analyze even my own feelings. Maybe a simple statement is the best answer: Balanchine is a genius; his masterpieces are incomparable; and that's that.

The New York City Ballet is twice blessed, for it also has Jerome Robbins. I danced there some of his most beautiful works—*Dances at a Gathering, Afternoon of a Faun*, and the two works he created for me, *Opus 19* and *The Four Seasons*. To work with Jerome Robbins is to work with a man totally committed, impassioned, and brilliant. He brings to you an incomparable gift in every rehearsal—his total presence.

And then there is the future. Who knows what the future holds? At the moment I enter a new phase with the Directorship of ABT. I know that the company's tradition of having a wide and varied repertoire of works from all over the world in all styles must be maintained. I also hope that I can bring a renewed sense of the classical style to the company and that it will continue to grow and prosper.

And I will dance, too. I can also hope that as a dancer I will continue to find the challenge, the excitement, the never-ending stimulation that has made my time in America so fantastic. The American people have been wonderful to me. They will get as much back as I can give.

MIKHAIL BARYSHNIKOV

***The Nutcracker*, American Ballet Theatre, 1976
Music, Peter Ilyitch Tchaikovsky; choreography,
Lev Ivanov, restaged by Mikhail Baryshnikov with
additional choreography by Vasily Vainonen**

Most people think of Tchaikovsky's *Nutcracker* as a light
divertissement for children. I have always felt, however, that
there is great pathos and tragic drama in the story of the toy
nutcracker that comes to life as a prince, and in this music,
too. It is music that can really stir the mind.

Rubies, from Jewels, New York City Ballet, 1978
Music, Igor Stravinsky;
choreography, George Balanchine

Balanchine has set this jet-age dance, the second act of *Jewels*, to Stravinsky's Capriccio for Piano and Orchestra. It has all the glamour and power of modern New York. It is American in a way that is timeless.

**A Chorus Line, from the ABC television special
"Baryshnikov on Broadway," 1980
Music, Marvin Hamlisch;
choreography, Michael Bennett**

Michael Bennett's *A Chorus Line* made a star of the Broadway "gypsy." These fantastic dancers have the most extraordinary range and flexibility. I was very lucky to be able to dance, if only briefly, in this work, one that changed the face of the Broadway musical...made the humanity of the gypsies' situation into a theatrical masterpiece.

***Airs*, The Paul Taylor Dance Company, 1979**
Music, George Frederick Handel;
choreography, Paul Taylor

In a work like *Airs*, Paul Taylor has created a unique and ineffable combination of abstract lyricism with underlying dramatic implications. *Airs* is an ensemble work that seems to flow joyously across the stage with effortless humanity, and yet there are hints of passion, sadness, ecstasy...so many different and wonderful *feelings*.

Theme and Variations, American Ballet Theatre, 1978
Music, Peter Ilyitch Tchaikovsky;
choreography, George Balanchine

Balanchine's *Theme and Variations* is a dance challenge in which two worlds meet and explode with star-bright power. This ballet is the marriage of the great Imperial Ballet tradition of the nineteenth-century master Marius Petipa (creator of *The Sleeping Beauty* and *Swan Lake*) and the extraordinary inventiveness of Balanchine, who brings his world-famous musicality and the apex of the neoclassical style together in one of the most exciting and pure works of twentieth-century choreography.

Mikhail Baryshnikov with his friend Sam

Being with animals is one of the joys of my life. Animals give
you love and a kind of devotion that has no equal in the
human world. They are ingenious and filled with humor and
above all with great dignity. They will always be a part of
my life.

Le Corsaire pas de deux, concert appearance, 1978
Music, Riccardo Drigo;
choreography, Marius Petipa

Bravura pas de deux like *Le Corsaire* are fun to do. They give the audience a chance to see ballet technique taken to the limit with great leaps and multiple spins. They have a kind of show-biz honesty that is very appealing. For the dancer they are both fun *and* a test. They are a test because you have to deliver all the excitement and still stay within the bounds of good taste and not go overboard.

The Four Temperaments, New York City Ballet, 1978
Music, Paul Hindemith;
choreography, George Balanchine

I really believe this to be one of Balanchine's great, great works, one that will live for ballet audiences forever. Set to a poignant and mysterious score by Paul Hindemith, *The Four Temperaments* seems to sum up a whole world, a world in which the inventions that Balanchine brought to ballet style are wedded to unforgettable dramatic images in ways that had never been done before or since. It was a rare privilege to dance this ballet.

***Orpheus*, New York City Ballet, 1979**
Music, Igor Stravinsky;
choreography, George Balanchine

Balanchine collaborated on this reworking of the Greek myth
with the celebrated sculptor Isamu Noguchi, who designed
the scenery and costumes. The ballet has simple but spec-
tacular effects that underline the artist's search for perfection
and the conflict between the affairs of the heart and the
affairs of the mind. Stravinsky's music has such variety and
such abundance of imagery that once heard it does not easily
leave the mind.

Prodigal Son, New York City Ballet, 1979
Music, Sergei Prokofiev;
choreography, George Balanchine

Prodigal Son was one of the legendary works created for Serge Diaghilev's Ballets Russes de Monte Carlo. The ballet has unforgettable settings and costumes by Georges Rouault and a searing dramatic score by Sergei Prokofiev. This was a work in which Balanchine gave the male dancer great prominence, and the role is an enormous challenge to any dancer who attempts it. Based on the traditional biblical story of the Prodigal Son, the work brilliantly captures the youthful enthusiasm of the young boy and his painful growth into manhood.

**Cabaret, from the ABC television special
"Baryshnikov on Broadway," 1980
Music, John Kander; choreography, Ron Field**

Making this television special was a unique experience for
me. It was my first attempt at doing an entire show as a
Broadway dancer. Ron Field created new versions of many
numbers from the famous Broadway shows for me. These
dances, all in the great American-musical tradition, exposed
me to a kind of theatrical dancing that I've always loved but
had never been able to perform... until this opportunity
came along. It was a pleasure from beginning to end, but
very, very hard. The special gift from Ron was the *Cabaret*
segment, his original choreography from the legendary
Broadway hit.

Giselle, **American Ballet Theatre, 1974**
Music, Adolphe Adam; choreography, Jean Coralli and
Jules Perrot, revised by Marius Petipa, staged for
American Ballet Theatre by David Blair

The great romantic classic *Giselle* was the first ballet I danced in America. As with all the great classics, it still holds fascination for me, even after my dancing the role of Albrecht hundreds of times. Dancing a work like *Giselle* is like going to the root of all the classical ballet tradition. It's like coming home, and at the same time you can always discover something new and challenging, as you do with a really valuable old friend.

***Fancy Free*, New York City Ballet, 1979
Music, Leonard Bernstein;
choreography, Jerome Robbins**

I was lucky enough to dance this role once, at a special New
York City Ballet Gala, and at that it was just a portion of this
American classic. But what an experience! All the wit and
stylishness of Jerome Robbins's brilliant choreographic signa-
ture, the sentiment and the gaiety, are with me still.

Don Quixote, American Ballet Theatre, 1978
Music, Leon Minkus;
choreography, Mikhail Baryshnikov,
after Marius Petipa and Alexander Gorsky

This was my second attempt at staging a full-length ballet for American Ballet Theatre. My version of *Don Quixote* is based on the traditional Russian one, but I tried to make it quick and bright, like an American Broadway show. Dancing the role of the young barber, Don Basilio, is great fun: it combines comic acting with bravura dancing.

***Petrouchka*, American Ballet Theatre, 1978**
Music, Igor Stravinsky; choreography, Michel Fokine;
scenery and costumes, Alexandre Benois

This is another of the great Diaghilev masterpieces that has
been preserved by American Ballet Theatre in a version that
was set by Fokine himself in the early 1940s. *Petrouchka* is
especially appealing because of its extraordinary crowd
scenes, at a typical Russian fair, and the deeply tragic story of
Petrouchka, who is a slave to his master, the puppeteer, and a
slave of his love for his fellow doll, the Ballerina. This was one
of Nijinsky's great roles, and it remains one of the great
challenges of the twentieth-century repertoire.

***Petrouchka*, American Ballet Theatre, 1978
Music, Igor Stravinsky; choreography, Michel Fokine;
scenery and costumes, Alexandre Benois**

The painted puppet, Petrouchka, is danced today in the
costume and makeup that Benois designed in 1911 for Nijinsky. The role demands psychological insights as well as the
ability to project them, and the face must be as expressive as
the body. Inside the straw doll a man is struggling to get out.

On vacation, Saint Barthélemy, French West Indies

What can I say about vacation? It's one of the ironies of a dancer's life that vacation is a necessary evil. Ideally a dancer should never stop working, refining the technique, keeping in top physical condition. But because of that constant pressure, to be on one of those fleeting vacations that come and go is like achieving nirvana.

The Steadfast Tin Soldier, **New York City Ballet, 1979**
Music, Georges Bizet;
choreography, George Balanchine

Balanchine is, of course, famous for his great neoclassical masterpieces. Many people forget that he has created many dramatic works. *The Steadfast Tin Soldier* is a bittersweet ballet staging of the Hans Christian Andersen fairy tale about the toy soldier who is in love with a toy doll. They have a chaste and delicious romance that ends in sadness as the doll is accidentally swept into the fireplace by an errant wind. This ballet was one of my favorites during my time at the New York City Ballet.

***Push Comes to Shove*, American Ballet Theatre, 1976**
Music, Joseph Lamb and Franz Joseph Haydn;
choreography, Twyla Tharp; costumes, Santo Loquasto

When I first came to America, I knew that there were many
challenges awaiting me as a dancer, but in my wildest imagination I couldn't have dreamed what was in store for me
with Twyla Tharp's *Push Comes to Shove*. Even though the
physical style of the dance is unique (it draws from American
social dancing, ballet, tap dancing, vaudeville routines, and
Miss Tharp's own inimitable technique), it is all held together
by a rigorous and "classical" intellect that molds all the wild
energy and humor into a powerful and coherent whole. *Push*
is one of the most exciting experiences I have ever had since I
came to America.

Santa Fe Saga, Eliot Feld Ballet, 1979
Music, Morton Gould; choreography, Eliot Feld

Working on this ballet was a departure for me. Feld created a
solo dance, something I have rarely performed. There is such
concentration and subtle invention in the piece that dancing
this work is like dancing ten others at the same time. I love
the Western imagery of the dance and its flickering moods.
Working with Feld was the realization of one of my dreams.
I love his ballets for their individuality and musicality.
He taught me a great deal.

Oklahoma!, from the ABC television special
"Baryshnikov on Broadway," 1980
Music, Richard Rodgers;
choreography, Ron Field

As I say in the show. "You know, I've been a Puppet in *Petrouchka*, a Slave in *Le Corsaire*, a Prince in *The Nutcracker*...but one thing I've never been is a full-fledged American cowboy with hat, boots, and everything." This was my big chance, in Field's restaging of the famous Rodgers and Hammerstein musical. And what a ball I had!

***Coppélia*, New York City Ballet, 1978**
Music, Léo Delibes; choreography, George Balanchine
and Alexandra Danilova, after Marius Petipa

One of the supreme pleasures in a ballet dancer's life is
dancing to great music. Delibes's score for *Coppélia* is one of
the best: not only does it have unforgettable melodies and
wonderful dramatic passages, but it is music meant for *dancing*. It has the rhythm and the shape that carry all the
classical *enchaînements* along with a zest and buoyancy that
make it a real joy to a dancer.

**_Prodigal Son_, New York City Ballet, 1979
Music, Sergei Prokofiev;
choreography, George Balanchine**

The Bible story of the Prodigal Son has had great appeal for
all the arts. Repentance and forgiveness are universal themes,
and the son's return to his father's house after he has been
broken by the world is one of the most dramatic scenes one
can portray—in ballet, in painting, or in sculpture.

Apollo, New York City Ballet, 1979
Music, Igor Stravinsky;
choreography, George Balanchine

Apollo is a work that changed the aspect of ballet in our time. It announced a new pared-down style that relied on the principles of unadorned classical technique but in a new mode which came to be called neoclassical. Dancing *Apollo* is like dancing in pure air. Everything in this work feels right. feels perfect. The challenge is in doing the steps as they are set, without any adornment, without special emphasis. If you can accomplish that, your own personality will shine through. *Apollo* is so very special that it stands alone—one of the landmarks in ballet history. To have danced it is for me an honor.

***Other Dances*, American Ballet Theatre, 1978**
Music, Frédéric Chopin;
choreography, Jerome Robbins;
costumes, Santo Loquasto

Jerome Robbins created *Other Dances* for me and for Natalia Makarova on the occasion of a special gala performance for the Library of Performing Arts at Lincoln Center. This work is one of the great highlights of my career in the West. Working with Robbins and seeing his unique musicality, his unique theatrical gifts, as he taught us the dance was an unforgettable experience. He gave me, in the period of creating *Other Dances*, such a deep understanding of his warmth and his passion that every time I dance this work *he* comes alive for me. *Other Dances* was a once-in-a-lifetime gift.

The Nutcracker, CBS television, 1977
Music, Peter Ilyitch Tchaikovsky;
choreography, Mikhail Baryshnikov
with additional choreography by Vasily Vainonen

This ballet about a Christmas-gift nutcracker that turns into
a handsome prince is one of the most popular in the world.
At Christmastime you can count on its being danced, in
different versions, by the leading ballet companies of many
countries.

Coppélia, New York City Ballet, 1978
Music, Léo Delibes;
choreography, Arthur Saint-Léon,
revised by George Balanchine and Alexandra Danilova

Unlike the princes and spirits in the romantic ballets, the characters in *Coppélia* are down-to-earth country youngsters who flirt and tease and have a good time. Franz is high-spirited but not very profound, and Delibes has given him delightful music to dance to.

***The Nutcracker*, CBS television, 1977**
Music, Peter Ilyitch Tchaikovsky;
choreography, Mikhail Baryshnikov
with additional choreography by Vasily Vainonen

Working in television has its peculiar problems. In a way you feel safe because you can do it over and over again. But to a dancer, naturally, it's never perfect. In the back of your mind you know that a final choice will have to be made and that choice is *it*, forever a record of that moment. And this can be frightening. On the other hand, film and television allow you to get many extraordinary theatrical effects that are not possible on the stage. You can expect the most unbelievable technical options, and get them.